A PALINDROME ANTHOLOGY
BY WILLIAM IRVINE

DO GEESE SEE GOD?

WITH ILLUSTRATIONS BY
STEVEN GUARNACCIA

SCHAFFNER PRESS
Tucson, Arizona

DO GEESE SEE GOD?

Portions of this book have been published previously in the following
volumes: "Madam I'm Adam" (1987); "If I Had A Hi-Fi" (1992);
and "Senile Felines/Calendar" (1991).

For Library of Congress Cataloging in Publication data,
contact the Publisher.

ISBN: 978-1943156-22-1
Adobe PDF: 978-1943156-23-8
Epub: 978-1943156-24-5
Mobi: 978-1943156-21-4

Printed in the United States of America

O.E.D. OR RODEO ?

The palindrome is the hothouse flower in the garden of wordplay.

There is something so aesthetically appealing about a word that reads the same backward as forward, particularly one like ANONANONA, which is—I'm sure you knew this—the Hawaiian word for ant. I have been interested in palindromes since childhood, when I discovered the mysterious connection between TUMS and SMUT. (It also helps to be able to read backward, a talent which I picked up from my mother.) This totally useless skill has led to a lifelong interest in collecting and inventing them.

The cult of the palindrome owes its existence to Sotades of Maroneia, a Greek poet and satirist of the third century B.C., who invented palindromic verse and coined the term. More recently, this century has produced J. A. Lindon and Leigh Mercer, British palindromists of rare accomplishment, and Dmitri Borgmann (1927-85), who not only created the term logology for the study of wordplay, but wrote lists of palindromic words as well as one of my favorite books, the delightful *Language on Vacation*. And the humorist James

Thurber was a part-time palindromist. One of his best: HE GODDAM MAD DOG, EH?

The secret to constructing a fine palindrome is to start with a promising middle word with well-spaced vowels and consonants (FELAFEL or ASPARAGUS or ARUGULA spring to mind) and build outward, rather than starting with an end word (a mistake common to tyros) and trying to work inward. Punctuation is suspended; the only poetic license. And only a small number of palindromes make any sense without a frame of reference. So, unless you know that you are reading a memo from a New Guinean decorator, R.E. PAPUA ETAGERE GATEAU PAPER doesn't mean much. Or AMARYLLIS SILLYRAMA (a discotheque for fancy flowers?). And how about SATAN, OSCILLATE MY METALLIC SONATAS? Proper names are traditionally a good source of palindromes. For some reason there are many involving Republicans and dictators. Consider the Sarah Palin-drome: WASILLA'S ALL I SAW. And others: DRAT SADDAM, A MAD DASTARD; WONDER IF SUNUNU'S FIRED NOW; NORIEGA CAN IDLE, HELD IN A CAGE-IRON; and my favorite, TO IDI AMIN: I'M A IDIOT. The real fun of a palindrome, of course, is its random celebration of the absurd.

Because most articles and prepositions are by definition excluded from the palindromic universe, there are an unusual number of examples that sound like sensational tabloid newspaper headlines. Hence, RAT IS SITAR and PART-SEMITE TIMES TRAP. Many of the most successful palindromes are remarkable in their brevity and simplicity: EVIL OLIVE, for example, or the heavenly GOLDENROD-ADORNED LOG. But all these pale in comparison to my all-time favorite, composed by the British author Alastair Reid:

> T. ELIOT, TOP BARD, NOTES PUTRID
> TANG EMANATING, IS SAD. "I'D
> ASSIGN IT A NAME: GNAT-DIRT
> UPSET ON DRAB POT TOILET."

The estimable Steven Guarnaccia and I are palindrome pals from way back. In fact, SO far back that when we first began our collaboration, the Internet was something in a galaxy far, far away. So in response to those children who say, "Can't you just look it up on the Internet?" I gently reply that many of my earliest efforts were actually the result of spending countless hours with pad and paper, thumbing through dictionaries and collecting word lists of likely suspects. Quaint, no?

Many of the most baroque palindromes could not be included here because they just had no use for the talents of Mr. Guarnaccia. How to do a drawing for KINNIKINNIK, an Indian smoking mixture made of bark and leaves? Or E. BORGNINE GRABS DAD'S GARDENING ROBE? SUPPOSITORY ROT: I SOP PUS is just disgusting. And then there's ON A CLOVER, IF ALIVE, ERUPTS A VAST, PURE EVIL: A FIRE VOLCANO (way too complicated). And the lovely I ROAMED UNDER IT AS A TIRED, NUDE MAORI (tough one). I could go on. But here, for your enjoyment, we present DO GEESE SEE GOD? and other plums of our palindromic plundering.

—WILLIAM IRVINE
April 2017

STELLA WON NO WALLETS

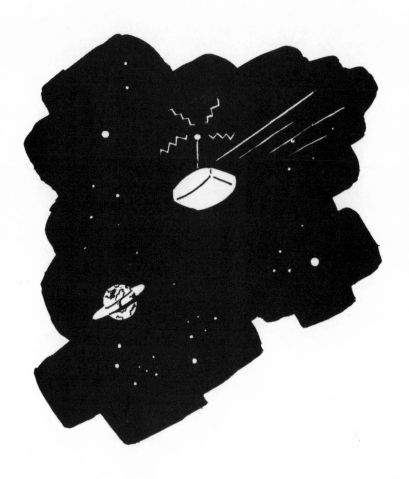

U.F.O. TOFU

NAMETAG GATEMAN

VIVA LE TE DE TEL AVIV

ROY, AM I MAYOR?

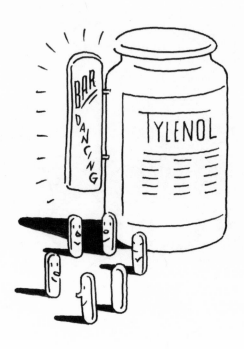

LONELY TYLENOL

EGAD! NO BONDAGE!

STAB NAIL AT ILL ITALIAN BATS

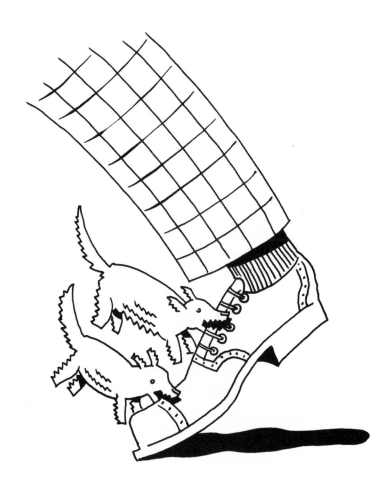

PETS NIP INSTEP

SNUG POPGUNS

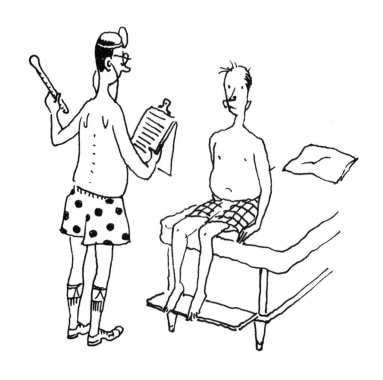

DR. AWKWARD

RENO LONER

SOME MEN INTERPRET NINE MEMOS

TRACI TORE EROTIC ART

YO, BANANA BOY

ENID AND EDNA DINE

WE SEVEN, EVE, SEW

NIGHT, FIFTH GIN

SAT IN A TAXI, LEFT FELIX AT ANITA'S

TUNA NUT

SARGE, I OFTEN ET FOIE GRAS

LIVE DADA DEVIL

REFLOG A GOLFER

REGINA A NIGER

DROWSY SWORD

MAYHEM, EH YAM?

SIT ON A POTATO PAN, OTIS!

DALLAS IS ALL AD

RED ROOTS TO ORDER

LAGER, SIR, IS REGAL

SEPARATE TAR APES

NURSE! I SPY GYPSIES! RUN!

OH, CAMERAS ARE MACHO

YAWN A MORE ROMAN WAY

A SANTA'S AT NASA

PAMELA'S ALE MAP

SENILE FELINES

IS SENSUOUSNESS I?

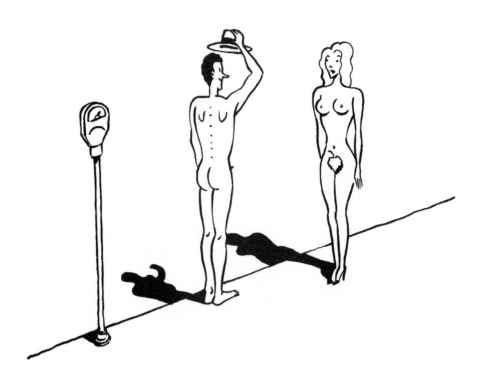

MADAM, I'M ADAM

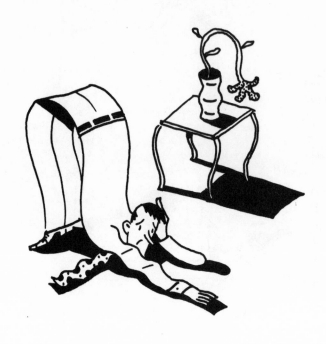

POOR DAN IS IN A DROOP

TRAFALGAR RAG: LA FART

RIO MEMOIR

SORE EYE, EROS?

"DESSERTS," I STRESSED

EGAD! AN ADAGE!

GODS RIDICULE LUCID I.R.S. DOG

TOO BAD, I BID A BOOT

WORM ROW

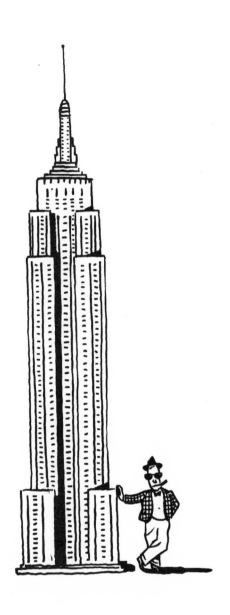

MUST SELL AT TALLEST SUM

NO WORD, NO BOND, ROW ON

MA IS A NUN, AS I AM

EVE IS A SIEVE

TRU-GOY YOGURT

NO LEMONS, NO MELON

OOLONG, NO LOO

LAY A WALLABY BABY BALL AWAY, AL

SLED AT ICE CITADELS

SEX AT NOON TAXES

GULP A SLAB O' BALSA PLUG

NOW NED, I AM A MAIDEN NUN;
NED I AM A MAIDEN WON

NAIL IT, PERT REPTILIAN!

NOG ERODED OREGON

TACO CAT

EROS? SIDNEY, MY END IS SORE

A GLORIA AIR, OLGA?

YELL UPSET A CIDER, PREDICATES PULLEY

PARMA HAM RAP

"M"LAB MENIAL SLAIN: EMBALM

SPIT Q-TIPS

GOD! A RED NUGGET! A FAT EGG UNDER A DOG!

POTS, NONSTOP

BIRD RIB

SEE? PURDAH HAD RUPEES

SLAP MY GYM PALS

LEPERS REPEL

LIB REGRETS BOLOGNA, MANGO, LOBSTER, GERBIL

DECADENT NED ACED

SNIFF 'UM MUFFINS

EEL GLEE

STOP! MURDER US NOT, TONSURED RUMPOTS!

ER…GODIVA, AVID OGRE

MAY A MOODY BABY DOOM A YAM?

A RAGA IN NIAGARA

SOLO GIGOLOS

OKIE'S SEIKO

BARCLAY ORDERED AN OMELETTE,
LEMONADE, RED ROYAL CRAB

A TIEPOLO, POLO, PIETA

NED, GO GAG OGDEN

STOLE COYOTE TOY, OCELOTS?

STRATAGEM: MEGATARTS

BOB, A NABOB

GUSTAV KLIMT MILK VATS—UG!

AMPLE HELP, MA?

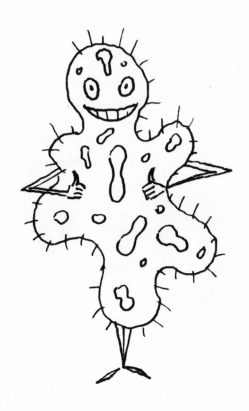

MR. EGO GERM

DIP IS NIL—INSIPID

PAGANINI DIN IN A GAP

SCRANTON'S TOTS NOT NARCS

EVIL OLIVE

TEPEE PET

SIS, SARGASSO MOSS A GRASS IS

UPDIKE KID—P.U.!

GNU DUNG

A GOTH SAW ADA WASH TOGA

AH, SATAN SEES NATASHA

DEGENERATE FETA RENEGED

ROCOCO "R"

MEGAWATT OTTAWA GEM

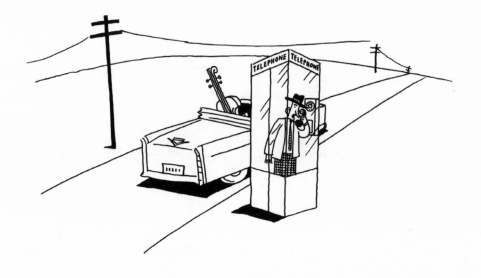

CALL IDA, COLLECT CELLO, CADILLAC

A DOG! A PANIC IN A PAGODA!

GAMEY EYE MAG

CAMUS SEES SUMAC

WE PANIC IN A PEW

STAR COMEDY BY DEMOCRATS

NEHRU FUR HEN

TANGO, O GNAT

DENIM AXES EXAMINED

TIT PECCADILLO DOLL? I'D ACCEPT IT!

STEP ON NO PETS

DISNEY YEN, SID?

DAEDALUS: NINE, PENINSULA: DEAD

SERIF FIRES

A SLUT NIXES SEX IN TULSA

CAIN, A MANIAC

NEVER ODD OR EVEN

RABBI BIB BAR

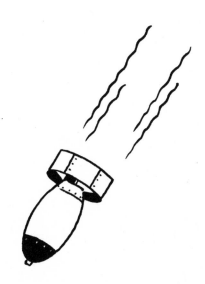

BOMBARD A DRAB MOB

IF I HAD A HI-FI

DAIRY MYRIAD

DIOR DROID

DRAW, OH COWARD!

LAMINATED E.T. ANIMAL

I MAIM MIAMI

SH, TOM SEES MOTHS!

DELIA SAILED, EVA WAVED, ELIAS AILED

NOSEGAY AGES ON

PARTY BOOBYTRAP

A MAN, A PLAN, A CANAL—PANAMA

MR. OWL ATE MY METAL WORM

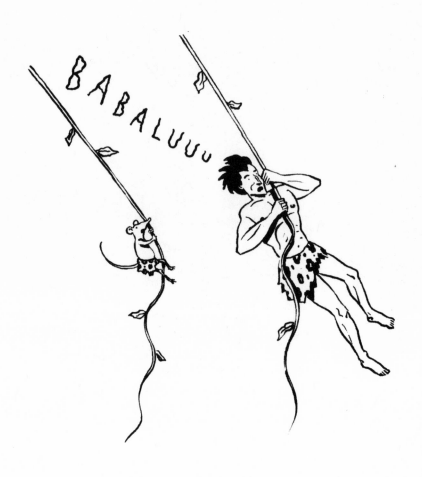

TARZAN RAISED DESI ARNAZ' RAT

KAYAK SALAD — ALASKA YAK

NAG A PAGAN

SEX-AWARE ERA WAXES

NEIL, AN ALIEN

I PREFER PI

DO GEESE SEE GOD?

William Irvine is an American logophile and writer whose work has appeared in many national magazines. A former senior editor at *House Beautiful*, he is the author of two previous collections of palindromes, *Madam I'm Adam* and *If I Had a Hi-Fi*. A native of Philadelphia, he now makes his home in North Carolina.

Illustrator Steven Guarnaccia, artist and designer, has authored and illustrated several books for children as well as collaborated with Mr. Irvine on the above palindrome collections. He is an Associate Professor of illustration at Parsons School of Design, and lives in Brooklyn, NY.